All About Erosion

Charmaine Robertson

Rosen REAL READERS

Rosen Classroom™
New York

Have you ever made a sand castle on the beach? Soon the **tide** rises and waves hit your castle. The water breaks the castle down and washes it away.

What happens to the castle is like erosion. Erosion is when wind, water, and weather break down soil and rock. It takes a long time.

The small pieces that break off are carried away. They are left behind somewhere else. A river **delta** is made this way.

Waves cause erosion on the shore. The waves break down stone and sand.

Rain causes erosion, too. Over time, small pieces of rock and soil break off. The rain carries them away.

The water in rivers causes erosion. It cuts slowly through the rock. The Grand Canyon is an example of this. It is in Arizona.

Wind is a strong force that causes erosion, too. These rocks in Utah were shaped by wind.

Glaciers also cause erosion. They move over land. As they move, they shape mountains and carve out valleys.

Erosion breaks down rock. The little bits of rock it makes are called **sediment**.

Erosion is part of the rock cycle. It is the process by which some rocks are formed. Over time, sediment builds up. It forms new rocks. Weather and erosion help form sedimentary rocks.

Glossary

delta A piece of land that is made of mud and sand at the mouth of a river.

glacier A large body of ice that moves slowly downward on land.

sediment Material such as sand and stone deposited by water, wind, or glaciers.

tide The regular upward and downward movement of the level of the ocean.